The Man From Galilee

Sermons And Orders Of Worship For Lent And Easter

Thomas A. Pilgrim

CSS Publishing Company, Inc.
Lima, Ohio

THE MAN FROM GALILEE

Scripture quotations are from the *Revised Standard Version of the Bible*, copyrighted 1946, 1952 ©, 1971, 1973, by the Division of Christian Education of the National Council of the Churches of Christ in the USA. Used by permission.

Library of Congress Cataloging-in-Publication Data

Pilgrim, Thomas A., 1944-
    The man from Galilee : sermons and orders of worship for Lent and Easter / Thomas A. Pilgrim.
        p.   cm.
    ISBN 0-7880-1131-6 (pbk.)
    1. Lent. 2. Lenten sermons. 3. Easter. 4. Easter—Sermons. 5. Jesus Christ— Sermons. 6. Sermons, American. 7. Worship programs.   I. Title.
BV85.B53   1998
264'.13—dc21   97-26626
                                                                            CIP

This book is available in the following formats, listed by ISBN:
    0-7880-1131-6   Book
    0-7880-1132-4   IBM 3 1/2
    0-7880-1133-2   Mac
    0-7880-1134-0   Sermon Prep

This book is dedicated to:

Alexandria Elizabeth Gray Pilgrim
Thomas Albert Pilgrim, III

Chandler Marie Foy

Justin Tanner Shirey
Joshua Tyler Shirey

They have brought our lives unspeakable joy

Preface

In February, 1997, I made my sixth journey to the Holy Land. I never tire of going there. In fact, these trips are for me times of rest and renewal. They keep me in touch with the roots and reality of our faith.

While the entire pilgrimage through the Holy Land is an inspiring journey, there are places which are more special than others. Bethlehem, the Garden of Gethsemane, and the empty tomb are some of these. For me there is also the area known in Bible times as "the Galilee." Galilee means, literally, "the district." It is a place of unrivaled beauty.

During the time of Jesus there were cities which surrounded the lake, what we call "the Sea of Galilee." Some of these cities had populations of 40,000 or more. So, it was a bustling area, through which ran the "via Maris," the main trade route from Egypt to the East.

Today the area is much more rural. But it is still easy to imagine what it was like in the time of Jesus. I especially love the ruins of the city of Capernaum. This city was the headquarters of Jesus. He made it His adopted home. It was the center of His ministry in Galilee, which is where He spent most of His three-year ministry. When I go to Capernaum I know I am in the place where Jesus lived, preached, taught, healed, and called disciples.

It was on one of these journeys that I first conceived of this series of messages for Lent and Easter on the Man from Galilee. I hope they will speak to those who read these pages and that they will see something of Him.

As always, I owe my wife Shirley a debt I could never pay for her encouragement and support in the ministry of preaching and writing.

Thomas A. Pilgrim
January 6, 1997

"Then Jesus came from Galilee ..."
Matthew 3:13

Table Of Contents

First Sunday In Lent   **11**
   Sermon: The Temptation Of His Life
   Prayer
   Children's Message
   Discussion Questions
   Order Of Worship

Second Sunday In Lent   **23**
   Sermon: The Transformation Of His Call
   Prayer
   Children's Message
   Discussion Questions
   Order Of Worship

Third Sunday In Lent   **35**
   Sermon: The Touch Of His Hand
   Prayer
   Children's Message
   Discussion Questions
   Order Of Worship

Fourth Sunday In Lent   **47**
   Sermon: The Treasure Of His Kingdom
   Prayer
   Children's Message
   Discussion Questions
   Order Of Worship

Fifth Sunday In Lent   **59**
    Sermon: The Test Of His Courage
    Prayer
    Children's Message
    Discussion Questions
    Order Of Worship

Palm Sunday   **71**
    Sermon: The Tragedy Of His Victory
    Prayer
    Children's Message
    Discussion Questions
    Order Of Worship

Easter Sunday   **83**
    Sermon: The Triumph Of His Defeat
    Prayer
    Children's Message
    Discussion Questions
    Order Of Worship

The Temptation Of His Life

Robert Penn Warren wrote a novel called *All The King's Men.* It was the story of a governor of Louisiana and his rise to power. His name was Willie Stark. At the end of his story he is shot down dead.[1] Here was a man who gained a kingdom and lost all he ever had.

Two thousand years earlier a man from Galilee said, "What would it profit a man if he gained the whole world and lost his soul?" Perhaps when He made that statement He was not only addressing it to those who heard Him, but also was looking back to a time of decision in His own life.

There is something so very curious about the man from Galilee. He has captivated the imaginations of people throughout twenty centuries. He transcends time and place, culture and custom, race and language. Something there is in Him that always speaks clearly to us. We see it throughout the gospels, everywhere He went, in everything He said and did. Son of God and Son of Man, we know He became one of us.

While He is the answer to all our struggles, we see Him struggling with the things He faced. And, as He finds the way for Himself He finds the way for us as well.

We see this truth at the very beginning of His ministry. He left His home up in beautiful Galilee, and went down the Jordan Valley to a place at the river. His cousin John the Baptist was there and he baptized Jesus in the river. And, a voice from Heaven said, "This is my beloved Son, in whom I am well pleased." Then, Matthew writes in the very next verse, the first of chapter four, "Then Jesus was led up by the Spirit into the wilderness to be tempted by the devil."

Immediately following His baptism Jesus faces the temptations, the greatest temptations of His life. The issue was not whether He would rule the world, but how He would take it. So, out there in

11

the wilderness of those barren Judean hills Jesus struggled with what He would do and how He would do it.

Sometimes we may not take this very seriously. We may not think Jesus was really tempted, not the way we are tempted, not our Jesus. But we need to understand that the temptations of Jesus were real temptations. Jesus was tempted. The New Testament clearly states this.

Matthew tells us plainly that Jesus was in the wilderness tempted by the devil. He did not say Jesus wondered, imagined, was charmed, or that He considered his options. He tells us He was tempted, and that He went there to be tempted.

Mark tells us He was tempted.

Luke tells us He was tempted.

John does not take time to mention it. He was in too big a hurry to get Jesus back up to Galilee.

However, the book of Hebrews tells us, "He was in all points tempted like as we are."

My wife Shirley and I have been to Jericho, not far from the place where Jesus was baptized by John the Baptist. You can stand there in Jericho and look up into the Judean hills to a place called the Mount of Temptation. It is easy to imagine Jesus being up there, by Himself, fasting for forty days, alone and hungry, struggling with what He would do and how He would do it.

Surely, He must have thought of some easy ways to do what He had to do. That was the temptation of His life.

So, there we see Him. He was tempted. Look at what He faced.

I.

Jesus was tempted by the wrong use of power. That was the first temptation. Matthew tells us the Tempter came to Jesus and said, "If you are the Son of God, command that these stones become bread." Then Matthew writes, "But He answered and said, 'It is written, Man shall not live by bread alone, but by every word that proceeds from the mouth of God.' " Jesus knew the answer was not in the wrong use of power. That would never relieve His hunger, for He must not live by bread, but by the word of God His Father.

Jesus understood that power He had. He knew how He could use this power. Here He was in a time of fasting, and the Tempter told Him He could use His power to get bread, to feed Himself.

What a temptation that must have been. But, Jesus knew He must not give in. He was not to use His power, the power God had given Him, to care for Himself, for any kind of personal gain or comfort.

Instead, Jesus found out how He was to use what God had given Him, the correct use of who He was and what He had.

Isn't this a temptation we face: the wrong use of who we are and what we have, the wrong use of what God has given us? I tell you that is a temptation which comes up before us every day.

God has blessed all of us abundantly.

A Sunday school teacher asked the children in her class what God had given the children of Israel to eat while they were in the wilderness. One little girl answered immediately, "Manna." The teacher said, "That's right, and what else?" After a long pause one boy replied, "Mountain Dew!"

God has blessed all of us. And, one of our temptations is how we use the power God has given us, who we are, and what we have.

The life, teachings, and examples of Jesus Christ all call us to the right use of who we are and what we have. We are called to respond the way Jesus did with the right use of all God has given us. And, we are called to do our best. That challenge always faces us.

It is said that General Stonewall Jackson once made this statement: "Do the best you can with what you have where you are."

Marshall Ney was one of Napoleon's commanders. When he had lost all of his men on the Russian front, he went back to see Napoleon. He told him he had tried and failed. Napoleon asked how he might know that he had done his best. Ney answered, "Sir, I would ask of you no more than I have done."[2]

Jesus asks no more of us than He has done Himself. It has to do with the right and best use of the power we possess, who we are, and what we have.

II.

Jesus was also tempted by the wrong way to popularity. That was the second temptation. Matthew tells us the Tempter came to Jesus and said, as he showed Him a view from the pinnacle of the Temple, "If you are the Son of God, throw yourself down; for it is written, 'He will give His angels charge of you,' and 'On their hands they will bear you up, lest you strike your foot against a stone.' " The temptation was to do something spectacular and win a following from that. But Jesus knew He could not do that, and Matthew tells us He replied, "It is written, 'You shall not tempt the Lord your God.' "

Jesus understood there were no shortcuts to easy popularity. Popularity and acceptance were not even what He sought. He sought only to serve His Father God, and establish His kingdom.

What a temptation that must have been. But Jesus knew He must not give in. He was not to seek this kind of popularity easily won.

Instead, Jesus found out how He was to go about His ministry, how He was to give Himself, and not hold Himself up. His Father God would do that later on the cross. He knew if He was lifted up in this way He would draw all people unto Himself.

Isn't this a temptation we face: the wrong way to popularity and acceptance? I tell you that is a temptation which comes up before us every day.

Sometimes we will do almost anything to gain popularity and acceptance.

A woman was all caught up in the Christmas rush. Finally, she had everything done on Christmas Eve, but then she remembered she had not sent cards to some people on one of her lists. She ran out to the store, bought fifty cards, came home and addressed and stamped 49 of them, and rushed to the post office to mail them. She came back home, and after dinner sat down for a moment and looked at the one card left over. She opened it and read the words on the inside, "This card is just to say a special gift is on the way." She had to spend the few days left in that week getting caught up.

Sometimes we would do anything to gain popularity and acceptance. Young people face it. We call it peer pressure. Adults

14

face it. We call it keeping up. But the call of God in our lives is not to do that. It is instead a call to be faithful followers who, like Jesus, seek to serve God and establish His kingdom.

One of the leaders of the early church was Polycarp, Bishop of Smyrna. He was brought to trial by the authorities and told he must renounce his Christian faith. He replied, "Fourscore and six years have I served Him, and He never did me wrong: how then can I revile my King, my Savior?" They took him out and put him to death. Later when the Christians wrote their history of that period they said, "Polycarp was martyred, Statius Quadratus being proconsul of Asia, and Jesus Christ being King forever!"[3]

We are called today to be the people who are faithful, who seek to serve God and His kingdom.

III.

Finally, Jesus was tempted by the wrong kind of partnership. That was the third temptation. Matthew tells us the Tempter came to Jesus and showed Him all the kingdoms of the earth and said, "All these things I will give you if you will fall down and worship me." But Jesus answered, "Begone, Satan! For it is written, 'You shall worship the Lord your God, and Him only you shall serve!' " Jesus knew He could never be partners with the devil. He could never compromise who He was and what He was about.

Jesus understood there could never be a partnership with the devil. He already had a covenant with His Father God. The Tempter told Him He could have the whole world. All Jesus had to do was worship him and He could take the world.

What a temptation that must have been. But Jesus knew He must not give in. He was to have no such partnership or compromise with anyone.

Instead, Jesus found out how He was to worship and serve His Heavenly Father.

Isn't that a temptation we face: the wrong kind of partnership and the compromise of who we are? We want a partnership sometimes instead of a covenant. I tell you that is a temptation which comes up before us every day.

So, we have to remember our covenant with God. And we have to hear the call of God to come and live in His covenant and be His children.

Do you know why Jesus made it through those temptations? It was because He remembered who He was. He had known it all along. And in between His Baptism and His temptations He had heard the voice of God: "This is my beloved Son, in whom I am well pleased." He never forgot it, the voice of His Father calling Him.

There was a boy whose behavior was terrible. But his mother noticed a change in him. He seemed to be making an effort to be thoughtful and kind. One day she decided to ask him what was going on. He said, "The other day at church the preacher put his hand on my head and said, 'You are a fine boy.' I knew he would be disappointed if he found out I wasn't, so I decided to try to be one." He never forgot it. It was like the voice of God calling him.

Harry Emerson Fosdick was one of the greatest American preachers of this century. He described his preaching as counseling on a large scale. Few people knew that as a young seminary student he reached the breaking point after working one summer in a New York Bowery mission. He went home and was overcome by deep depression. One day he stood in the bathroom with a straight razor to his throat. He thought about taking his own life. And then — and then he heard his father in the other room calling his name, "Harry! Harry!"[4] It called him back. He never forgot it. It was like the voice of God calling him.

So I want to remind you today that in those times when you are in the wilderness, trying to find your way through, and when temptation comes and offers you the wrong answer, the wrong choice — the wrong use of power, the way to popularity, the wrong kind of partnership — then you remember that God has called your name: "This is my beloved son, my beloved daughter, in whom I am well pleased." And, you remember that because God has called your name He will see you through.

_____

16

1. Robert Penn Warren, *All The King's Men* (Random House: New York, 1960), p. 131.

2. Ernest A. Fitzgerald, *Keeping Pace: Inspirations In The Air* (Pace Communications Inc.: Greensboro, North Carolina, 1988), p. 14.

3. James S. Stewart, *The Wind Of The Spirit* (Abingdon Press: Nashville and New York, 1968), p. 55.

4. Robert Moats Miller, *Harry Emerson Fosdick* (Oxford University Press: New York and Oxford, 1985), p. 44.

O God, our Father, who created us to be Thy children and called us to be Thy people, accept our worship today as we call upon Thee, our help, our hope, our strength and shield.

Here at the beginning of this season of Lent we know we begin a journey which will carry us with Thy Son along the way of the cross. As we journey with Him may we come to know all He suffered through, for He was tempted as we are, and today we remember the temptations of His life.

We thank Thee, gracious God, for all Thy blessings upon us, for Thy merciful hand at work in our lives, and for Thy goodness we see surrounding us in so many ways.

And as we thank Thee, Father, we express our gratitude by giving ourselves back to Thee as we seek to be Thy children in every way and serve Thee as the people of God. Enable us to follow after the example of Thy Son and our Savior Jesus Christ.

Mold us, shape us, make us into Thy own image so that we will not make Thee into our images. Forgive us, redeem us, empower us, and give us great visions so that we would give ourselves to Thee.

Finally, Lord, we ask that, whatever our life situation, whatever our own individual calling, Thou would give us a sense of belonging to the great family of God, that we may be young in commitment, mature in service, and growing older in our faith in Thee.

Bless the sick and sorrowful of our church and community and all the great people of the world, for we pray in the name of Christ. Amen.

The Boy And The Apples

Good morning, boys and girls. I am so glad you have come to worship today. It is good to see all of you here.

Today is a really special day. It is the First Sunday in the season of Lent. This is a time that leads up to Easter Sunday. On these Sundays we are thinking about Jesus going toward Jerusalem, and the things He did along the way.

Now, look at this apple. It's a good-looking apple, isn't it? I bet it would taste really good.

One time a boy about your age went to the store. He was standing at the door looking at a big barrel of apples. The man who ran the store saw him. He walked over to the boy and said, "Son, are you trying to steal an apple?" The little boy answered, "No, sir. I'm trying to keep from it."

In our scripture lesson today we will read about what we call the temptations of Jesus. Who knows what the word "temptation" means? One way to put it is this. It is seeing a way or an opportunity to do something that is wrong. It is thinking about doing something we should not do.

Jesus was tempted not to be as good as God made Him to be.

Sometimes all of us are tempted to do something God would not want us to do. There is a way for us to handle that. And that is to ask God to help us. We can ask God to help us remember to be the boys and girls He wants us to be. We are His children and He is our Father. And He wants us to be like Him and live like His Son Jesus.

So, when you are tempted to do something that is wrong, ask God to help you do what is right. And God will do just that. He will help you.

Let's bow our heads for our time of prayer. Father, help us always to do the things you want us to do and to remember we are your children. In Jesus' name we pray. Amen.

Discussion Questions
Lent 1

1. Begin with a prayer led by a member of the group.

2. Have someone read Matthew 4:1-11.

3. Having asked them ahead of time, let members of the group share various sections of the chapter.

4. What is the significance of this time for Jesus?

5. What were the things Jesus was tempted to do?

6. How did Jesus face these temptations?

7. What are the things which tempt us today?

8. How do we overcome these temptations?

9. Close with each person saying a sentence prayer and then a benediction by the leader.

Order Of Worship

11:00 a.m.   **First Sunday In Lent**

WE GATHER TO WORSHIP GOD
Prelude

Chiming the Hour

Introit

Greeting
Leader: Come now, let us reason together, says the Lord;
People: Though your sins are like scarlet, they shall be like snow.

Hymn of Praise   "Lift High The Cross"

Affirmation of Faith   The Apostles' Creed

Welcome and Sharing

Children's Message   "The Boy And The Apples"

WE TURN TO GOD IN PRAYER
Joys and Concerns

Morning Prayer and the Lord's Prayer

WE GIVE TO GOD
Prayer of Dedication

Offertory

Doxology

21

WE HEAR GOD'S WORD

Hymn of Preparation   "Fairest Lord Jesus"

Anthem

Reading of the Scriptures   Matthew 4:1-11
Leader: This is the Word of the Lord.
People: Thanks be to God.

The Message   "The Temptation Of His Life"

WE RESPOND TO GOD

The Invitation to Christian Discipleship

Hymn of Invitation   "O Love That Wilt Not Let Me Go"

Benediction

Congregational Response

WE DEPART TO SERVE GOD

Postlude

The Transformation Of His Call

In preparation for our mission trip to Puerto Rico in the summer, several of us went there in the spring to see the camp where we would be working. When we got there we met some people from several churches in Alabama who were working at the camp that week. They shared their food with us that evening, and then after the meal we met for a time of singing and devotion. Between the meal and the devotion time I looked around some and found a bookcase. I looked at several books and found one called *Who Is Jesus?* I flipped through the pages and saw a chapter with the title, "Did Jesus Really Exist?" That chapter examined much of the historical records. Some of them said yes and others said no.

Later in the evening as I sat in a circle with those people I did not really know, I thought about the question in the book. We were on a large porch off the dining hall. There we were from different backgrounds on the side of a mountain in Puerto Rico among other people whose ways and language were unknown to us. Yet, something had brought all of us together. Something had caused us to be there. We had come there because of Jesus in His name to serve Him. Something about that united us and made friends of strangers. I remember thinking about the question, "Did Jesus really exist?" And I answered it in my mind, "Only Jesus could cause this to happen."

From the beginning there was always something about Jesus which drew people to Him. There was something in His manner, something about His look, something in His eyes which must have reached out and captivated people who saw Him.

One day, not long after returning to Galilee from the Jordan Valley, Jesus walked along the shore of the Sea of Galilee. There He saw two fishermen, Simon and Andrew. It is thought by some scholars that those two brothers had been followers of John the

Baptist. If so, perhaps they were at the river when Jesus was baptized. At any rate, it is possible that Jesus knew who they were, and that they may have known something of Him. We will never know this. But Matthew does tell us that when Jesus saw the two fishermen He stopped for a moment and said to them, "Follow me, and I will make you fishers of men." Then Matthew tells us they followed Jesus. Without hesitation they followed Jesus and became His disciples.

The three of them walked further along the northern shore of the lake until they came to other fishermen, James and John. Jesus called them also to become disciples. They made the same response as the first two, and they also followed Jesus immediately.

The lives of those fishermen were never the same. It was true of all those men and women, young people and children who came under the influence of the life of Jesus. The call of Jesus transformed them, and nothing was ever the same.

This has been true throughout the ages. Everywhere the name of Jesus has been spoken life is different, better, higher, nobler. We have found it to be true for us as well. Our lives are better because of the transforming call of Jesus.

So today, with this in mind, would you remember these things about this encounter Jesus had with the fishermen?

I.

First, Jesus saw their true talent. He knew what they were capable of doing. He saw the true talent they had. Matthew writes that when Jesus walked by the Sea of Galilee He "saw two brothers, Simon called Peter, and Andrew his brother, casting a net into the sea; for they were fishermen."

Why would Jesus choose fishermen to be His disciples? William Barclay, the renowned Bible scholar, wrote a book some years ago called *The Mind of Jesus*. He said that Jesus chose fishermen because they were "the kind of men" He needed. Fishermen had the qualities Jesus needed in His disciples. Barclay says they possessed the qualities of closeness to God, courage, patience, and wise judgment.[1]

So, what we have here is a carpenter turned preacher who chooses fishermen to help Him build a church and a kingdom, and fill them up with people drawn together with the great net of God's love. Jesus knew they could help Him do this, for He saw their true talent. He looked beyond what was obvious to all, that they were fishers of fish, and deeper than what was seen on the surface, rough men weathered by the sun and the wind. Jesus looked at those inner qualities, the real nature of those men, and He knew what stalwart, courageous, daring men they could become.

Of course, you see quickly now the implications of this kind of thinking. You know where I am headed with this, and you know what I am about to say. If Jesus could use their talent, He can also use ours, for He has seen us.

A man applied for a job with a transport company. During the training course the instructor said, "Suppose you are going down a mountain road and your truck is out of control. Your brakes have failed. A car is in front of you, and another truck is coming up the mountain in the other lane. What would you do?" He replied, "First thing I would do is wake up my partner, Leroy." The instructor asked, "Why would you do that?" And the man said, "Because Leroy is just an old country boy, and he's never seen a wreck like that before."

Who knows what could happen when Jesus has seen us. When Jesus looked at the fishermen, they did not know how He would use them. But they also looked back at Jesus. When we look back at Jesus, we see the reflection of what we can become, and what He can do with what we have.

When the London preacher Charles Spurgeon was fifteen years old he was headed to church one Sunday. But the snow was so deep he could not go on. Instead he stopped in at a little Methodist church. The pastor was not able to get there, so one of the members spoke to the small congregation. He quoted the verse, "Look unto me and be ye saved, all the ends of the earth." He really did not have much to say, but he kept quoting the words, "Look unto me, and be ye saved." Finally, he looked at the young man and said, "Young man, look to Jesus. Look, look, look!" Charles Spurgeon wrote years later, "I looked and suddenly the cloud was gone. The darkness was rolled away and for the first time in my life I saw the sun."[2]

Jesus saw the fishermen and they saw Him. Jesus and the fishermen got a glimpse of their true talent.

II.

Second, Jesus said the word that transforms. He knew how to enable them to do what they were capable of doing. He knew how to transform them. Matthew writes that Jesus said to them, "Follow me, and I will make you fishers of men."

No longer would they be fishing for fish. Now they would be fishing for people. They would use their talent for fishing and the qualities which made them fishermen to begin catching people. Jesus transformed them: "I will make you fishers of men."

Jesus spoke transforming words to many people. Later on, near the end of His life, He would finally say to Simon, "You are Peter (meaning the rock) and upon this rock I will build my church." To another He said, "Your sins are forgiven, take up your bed and go home." And, to another He said, "Go and sin no more." In so many places and to so many people Jesus spoke transforming words, "You will ... You are ..."

Those are the words He speaks to us today: "Follow me, and I will make you fishers of men." A part of that following means learning His way. Jesus trained the twelve for three years before they were ready. A disciple was a student. He was getting them ready. And still they were not ready. They knew they were not ready, but He was ready.

Sometimes learning is difficult.

A little boy went off for his first day at school. He was the terror of the neighborhood, and his mother knew it. She wondered how he would do. When he came in she asked him if he had cried. He said, "No, but the teacher sure did."

In the church we are in school. It is the "Jesus Training School," the "You Shall Be School," the "Be Not Conformed To This World, But Be Transformed By The Renewal Of Your Mind School." And in this training school we are being transformed.

One American leader was asked what person had the most influence on his life. He said it was a teacher he had in school who said to him, "You can do better than this." The words stayed with him all his life.

Jesus said those transforming words to the fishermen, and He transformed them.

III.

Third, Jesus set them to their task. He knew how to motivate them to enable them to do what they were capable of doing. Matthew writes that "they immediately left their nets and followed Him."

These fishermen, who would now be fishing for people, were motivated by Jesus to go with Him, be trained by Him, and allow Him to set them to their task. Even as they were learning they were beginning to serve. Jesus would send them out to preach the Good News, and He would begin to depend upon them. Already they were on their way to being not only disciples but also apostles, servants, witnesses, and representatives.

That is our calling today. That is the task at hand for us — to be a church and to be individuals who major in discipleship. We are to be disciples, people who serve, witness, believe, hope, give, and represent Christ.

William Temple, a Christian leader earlier in this century, said, "Christ wrote no book; He left in the world as His witnesses a body of men and women on whom His spirit came."[3]

G. Ray Jordon, Methodist preacher from North Carolina and teacher of preachers at Emory University, wrote years ago, "The hope of civilization is that we shall be able to produce enough Christlike men to save it."[4]

That is the world's only hope. It was when Jesus first walked along the Sea of Galilee. It still is today.

Kenneth Wyatt became famous for his paintings of horses. He has since become better known among church people for his paintings of the disciples. When he was working on those portraits he went into a truck stop to eat. He sat down at a counter, and he and

27

a truck driver struck up a conversation. They introduced themselves and the truck driver said, "Oh, you're the guy who paints horses." As they talked, the truck driver asked him what he was working on, and Kenneth Wyatt told him he was painting the disciples. Then he asked the truck driver if he would be willing to pose for one of those portraits. When he answered yes Kenneth Wyatt said to him, "From now on you are Thomas."

I do not know what happened after that, who the truck driver was, or what this might have meant to him. But can you imagine what it might mean to you to hear the words, "From now on you are a disciple"?

Those words transformed the fishermen. And those words have transformed us as well. May all of us continue in the transformation as we give our lives to Him who said, "Follow me, and I will make you fishers of men."

---

1. William Barclay, *The Mind of Jesus* (Harper & Row Publishers: New York and Evanston, 1960), p. 65.

2. Walter L. Underwood, *The Contemporary Twelve* (Abingdon Press: Nashville, 1984), p. 48.

3. Elton Trueblood, *The Incendiary Fellowship* (Harper & Row Publishers: New York, Evanston, and London, 1967), p. 78.

4. G. Ray Jordon, *The Emerging Revival* (Abingdon-Cokesbury: New York and Nashville, 1946), p. 139.

O God, our creator, sustainer, redeemer and friend, who has blessed us all our days with good gifts too numerous even to begin to list, accept the worship and praise and thanksgiving we offer to Thee.

On these Sundays, O God, as we follow Jesus on the way of the cross, help us to remember He still calls us to meet Him there. And remind us that our lives are transformed as we give up all to follow Him.

Father, for all of Thy goodness, for the bounty of Thy hand, we thank Thee. And we seek to be blessed by Thee in even greater ways. Give us a greater strength of purpose, a larger vision, a greater hope and faith that will see us through.

Help us, Father, to be like Thy Son. Help us to be brave, strong, kind, loving, merciful, understanding, and patient. And help other people to be patient with us, for sometimes we try even Thy patience.

Bless the work, the mission, and ministry of this church. Enable us to be all Thou hast called us to become. Help us to dream great dreams and to attempt great deeds for Thee and the Kingdom of our Lord and Savior Jesus Christ.

Bless the great people of the world and all who suffer. Bless the great people of Jerusalem and give them Thy peace.

Be with those of our own church family and our various communities who are sick and who suffer in any way. Bring comfort and help to them all.

Hear these our prayers today, for we make them in the name of Thy well-beloved Son, who still leads us to pray. Amen.

Only A Phone Call Away

Good morning. I'm so glad to see you today. And I'm so glad you have come to church.

I want to show you a telephone today. Actually we call this a cell phone. With this phone you can call anyone in the world from anywhere in the world. You can use this phone in your car, which is what many people do with these phones.

I remember seeing a television commercial one time which had this line in it: "only a phone call away." Anybody anywhere is only a phone call away.

A phone call can change your life. Maybe someone calls and says, "It's a boy!" or "It's a girl!" Maybe they call and say, "I have a prize for you!" Maybe they call and say, "Come to my party."

Long ago Jesus called some people and it changed their lives. It happened many times. He did not call them on the phone, of course. But He spoke to them and asked them to follow Him. The Bible says He called them, meaning He asked them to be His disciples. And they agreed to go with Him, to follow Him. They did become His disciples. That changed their lives.

He still calls us to follow Him. He wants us to believe in Him, to love Him, to follow Him, to be His disciples still today.

When we say yes to Jesus it changes our lives forever. It makes our lives better than they would ever be any other way. To live with Jesus and for Jesus is the best kind of living. So, I hope you will say yes to Jesus. It will make your life all you want it to be. Thanks for being with us today.

May we pray. O God, we thank you for your Son, Jesus Christ, and that He has called us to follow Him. We pray in His name. Amen.

Discussion Questions
Lent 2

1. Ask someone to begin the session with a prayer.

2. Have someone read Matthew 4:18-22.

3. Having asked them ahead of time, let members of the group share various sections of the chapter.

4. How did Jesus call His followers?

5. What was He calling them to do?

6. What did this mean to them?

7. What has the call of Jesus meant in your life?

8. How do we continue to hear His call?

9. Ask each person to reflect quietly about answering the call of Jesus today. Then, pray together the Lord's Prayer with the leader giving the benediction.

Order Of Worship

11:00 a.m.   Second Sunday In Lent

WE GATHER TO WORSHIP GOD

Prelude

Chiming the Hour

Introit

Greeting
Leader: Come, let us walk in the light of the Lord,
People: That He may teach us His ways and that we may walk
         in His paths.

Hymn of Praise   "All Hail The Power Of Jesus' Name"

Affirmation of Faith   The Apostles' Creed

Welcome and Sharing

Children's Message   "Only A Phone Call Away"

WE TURN TO GOD IN PRAYER

Joys and Concerns

Morning Prayer and the Lord's Prayer

WE GIVE TO GOD

Prayer of Dedication

Offertory

Doxology

32

WE HEAR GOD'S WORD

Hymn of Preparation   "Make Me A Captive, Lord"

Anthem

Reading of the Scriptures   Matthew 4:18-22
Leader: This is the Word of the Lord.
People: Thanks be to God.

The Message   "The Transformation Of His Call"

WE RESPOND TO GOD
The Invitation to Christian Discipleship

Hymn of Invitation   "When I Survey The Wondrous Cross"

Benediction

Congregational Response

WE DEPART TO SERVE GOD
Postlude

The Touch Of His Hand

A little girl named Charlotte went with her grandmother on a shopping trip downtown. When she returned home her parents were talking with her about the trip, what she had seen, how she liked it. They asked her if she had been afraid among all those people and cars as she crossed the street. She said, "No. The big policeman held up his strong hands and all the cars stopped and Charlotte crossed over."

Jesus the carpenter had hands bronzed by the sun, strong hands. And with those great, strong hands He came to be the hands of God lifting up a fallen humanity.

Early in His ministry Jesus was in the Decapolis, the ten cities around the eastern shore of the Sea of Galilee. The people brought to Jesus a man who was deaf and dumb, and "they begged Him to put His hand on him." Later Jesus healed a boy possessed by a spirit which caused him to fall on the ground. Jesus "took him by the hand and lifted him up." A woman was brought to Jesus and accused of adultery by a mob. But Jesus knelt down and with His hand wrote in the sand. When they put Jesus to death they drove great nails through those hands of mercy and kindness. When he rose from the tomb He said to His disciples, "Behold my hands." And, when He left them, "He lifted His hands and blessed them."

Then we read this passage from Matthew's gospel. Jesus was at His headquarters for His Galilean ministry, the city of Capernaum. While staying in that city He had a room in the home of Simon Peter, the fisherman. That house was located only about a block away from the synagogue. So it was a convenient place for Jesus to stay.

Matthew tells us that after Jesus had delivered the Sermon on the Mount near Capernaum, He came back to town where He met a Roman centurion. This man asked Jesus to heal his servant. When

Jesus agreed to go to his home, the man said, "Lord, I am not worthy that you should come under my roof. But only say the word, and my servant will be healed." Jesus marveled at this man's faith, and said, "Not even in Israel have I found such faith" (Matthew 8:10b). And, He said to the centurion, "Go; be it done to you as you have believed" (Matthew 8:13a).

Then Jesus and Simon Peter went home. When they got there they discovered Simon's mother-in-law was sick with a high fever. Jesus went into her room, and Matthew gives us these two sentences to describe what happened: "And He touched her hand, and the fever left her. Then she rose and served them."

In those few words Matthew tells us so much about what Jesus did for people everywhere, and what He still does. It is very simple, and simply this.

I.

The touch of His hand cured her sickness. His hand cooled her head. We know very little about this person. We know her illness was not something permanent. It was a high fever. We do know Jesus saw that she was sick with this fever. No one had to tell Him, or ask Him to go do anything about it. Jesus did what He always did. He responded to the human situation, the human need. He touched her hand with His hand, "and the fever left her."

The touch of His hand still cures us. Sometimes it is a physical illness. There are many examples of people who have been healed of some physical illness when the doctors saw no cure. And many times the doctors have said, "This is not my doing." Sometimes it is not the touch of any human hand, but the touch of God's hand.

Sometimes it is an emotional illness, an illness of the mind. Barbara Brokhoff told about a lady who is listed in the book, *Who's Nobody In America.* Her name is Mildred. She has been under the care of her therapist for a number of years. But he still calls her Sarah.[1] No wonder she was in therapy. Sometimes that is where we need God's touch.

Sometimes it is an illness in relationships. The headlines are full of it every day: strife between nations, groups, classes, races, families, individuals. All the world needs the touch of God's hands.

Whatever it is, none of us are immune from various kinds of illnesses. All of us live all the time in a danger zone.

A man who lived out in L.A. had an unhealthy fear of driving on the freeway. He refused to do it. He talked with his doctor about it. His doctor said, "You need to break out of this fear which cripples your life. Go out there at some time of the week when it is safe. Try it at 11:00 a.m. on Sunday morning. The Protestants will be in church, the Catholics will be at mass, and the Jews will be on the golf course since the Sabbath is over." So the next Sunday he tried it. He pulled out onto the freeway at exactly 11:00 a.m., and was run over by a Seventh-Day Adventist.

Life is dangerous for all of us. And because it is, we still need the touch of His hand to cure our illnesses, to cool our heads, to shape and reshape us, to mold and mend us.

In his book, *The Power of Holy Habits,* William H. Hinson wrote about the painter who said to a carpenter, "Do your best and I will caulk the rest."[2]

We still need the touch of His hand to cure what is wrong with us.

II.

The touch of His hand made her steady. His hand put her on her feet. Matthew writes that the fever left her, and "then she arose." Jesus put her back on her feet and made her steady. No longer was she weak and disoriented. Now she was in control.

The touch of His hand still makes us steady. My goodness, we need that today.

One Sunday I heard some parents coming into Sunday school. One mother said, "We were talking about what state we live in, and my youngest said we live in a state of confusion."

Many of us do these days. Many of us are caught up in a whirl-wind of constant activity. I heard about one Methodist preacher who was so busy he wore his suits out from the inside.

Living in such times we need something to hold us steady. We need the hand of God because of everything going on around us.

We need the hand of God to hold us steady. The steady hand of God will enable us to get back on our feet in the face of all the things which would overwhelm us and in spite of life's disappointments, many of which have the power to flatten us out. We need the steady hand of God in our lives and the steadying influence of Christ. Saint Paul urges us, "Therefore take up the whole armor of God, that you may be able to withstand in the evil day, and having done all, to stand."

Then when we stand, we discover the miracle which has taken place. When Jesus enables us to stand, then we stand for God.

In one of his books Dr. Wallace Chappell tells the story of William Carey, who has been called the father of the modern missionary movement. When he was young he attended a meeting at his church and asked a question about people in the world who had not been converted. Someone said, "Young man, sit down. If the Lord wishes to convert the heathen, He will do it." Wallace Chappell wrote that he sat down, "but the day came when he stood up."[3] And when he stood up, he became a great missionary for God.

When Jesus enables us to stand, we find ourselves standing for Him. We still need His hand to make us steady. That brings us simply to this.

III.

The touch of His hand enabled her to serve. His hand put her hands to work. Matthew writes that she "served them." Now back on her feet, she served those who were there.

The touch of His hand still enables us to serve. That is the only motive for giving ourselves to the Church of Christ and the Kingdom of God. There is no other reason for us being here.

Carlyle Marney, the great Baptist preacher, said, "The reaction to who he is puts us in church always."[4]

Not only does it put us in Christ's church, it also puts Christ's church in us. It does something to the way we look at life. It gives us a different set of values. It makes us want to be servants.

The touch of the hand of Christ upon us gives us a different understanding of our own hands. Hands which could be used for taking become hands used for giving. Hands which could be used for hoarding become hands used for sharing. Hands which could be used for holding down become hands used for lifting up. How will you use your hands?

There were two young men who wanted to become artists. Neither of them had the money to go to school. While both of them wanted to paint, one of them knew the other clearly had more talent. So he offered to work while his friend went to school. The student studied and learned, while the other worked long and hard in the heat of the sun. With the passing of time the hands of the artist became skilled, while the hands of the laborer became scarred. One night the artist saw his friend sitting by a window praying. And he decided to paint those hands which had been sacrificed so his skill could be perfected. Today we call them "The Praying Hands." Hands turned down to the sod and turned up to God have now become an inspiration to millions. How will you use your hands?

When I was a boy I was impressed by the stories my father told in his sermons. Perhaps I was not even aware at the time of the impression they made upon me, but I still remember many of them today.

I remember him telling about a young woman who was a servant for a wealthy family. There was an invalid in that home and she took care of that person. She was a devoted Christian, but rarely was she ever able to attend church and serve God through the church. She was often concerned about this. She became seriously ill, and it was learned that she had an illness from which she would not recover. The minister came to see her, and they talked about her illness and her faith. She expressed her concern about her lack of involvement in her church, and how little she had done. She asked the minister how Jesus would even know her name. He put his hand upon hers and said, "Just show Him your hands." Her hands had become for some other person the hands of God — and God would know her by those hands.

Would you open your life to the touch of the Master's hand so that He would be able to use your hands?

---

1. Barbara Brokhoff, *Trouble on the Mountain* (CSS Publishing Co., Inc.: Lima, Ohio, 1986), p. 14.

2. William H. Hinson, *The Power of Holy Habits* (Abingdon Press: Nashville, 1991), p. 70.

3. Wallace Chappell, *The Trumpet's Certain Sound* (Wallace Chapel Ministries: Nashville, 1987), p. 44.

4. Carlyle Marney, *The Carpenter's Son* (Abingdon Press: Nashville and New York, 1967), p. 52.

Morning Prayer
Lent 3

Almighty God, our Heavenly Father, we come before Thee to-day with thanksgiving and songs of praise for all Thou hast done for us, with us and in us.

We come seeking the touch of Thy hands upon us and the touch of Christ, who came to be the expression of Thy love in this world. In this time of the year we remember how He touched the lives of hurting humanity all across Galilee, in cities and towns, highways and byways. And we know He came for us as well.

We thank Thee for this, O God, and for the wonders of Thy creation, for the beauty of the world, the rising of the sun in the east and the setting of the sun in the west. We thank Thee for the flowers of the field, the birds of the air, and every living thing. We are thankful for the gift of life, and that Thou hast created us in Thine own image to be like Thee, to be Thy children, to be heirs of Thy kingdom.

Continue to bless us with gifts of love, mercy, and grace. We ask not for the things we want, but only for the things we need. Thou knowest them. Give us the willingness to serve, to help, to heal, to hope. Give us all the faith we need, and we need a lot. Give us the willingness to forgive and forget, for unless we do both we have done neither.

Bless our church family. Bless our children and youth, for they are precious to Thee and to us. Bless our families and those among us with no families near. Bless our sick, those in sorrow, and those who are troubled. Make them whole. We make this our prayer in the name of Him who is all things to us. Amen.

Give Him Your Hand

I am so glad to see each of you here this morning. Today I want each of you to hold up your hands. Look at them really good. We can all do a lot of good with our hands.

Today in our scripture lesson we will read about Jesus touching a person's hands and then lifting her up with His hand. The touch of Jesus' hand made many people well.

Hands are still important. Today we shake hands with people we meet. Sometimes we will pat someone on the back with our hand when we want to congratulate them or wish them well. The American Indians would greet another person by holding up one hand. Sometimes we wave at another person across the street.

Still, the best thing all of us can do is to give our hands to Jesus. A number of years ago there was a popular song which was played often on the radio about this very thing. The song was "Put your hand in the hand of the man who stilled the water."

The hands of Jesus will help you today. He will still the waters when you feel like you are caught up in a storm at sea. He will take you by the hand and lift you up. He will put His hand on you when you are afraid. He will help you find your way when you feel like you are lost.

So, I want to ask all of you to give Him your hand. Now, let us all hold each other's hands. Do you see how close our hands are? We are all together, holding hands and holding on. You hold onto Jesus just this tight, because He is holding onto you.

May we pray. O God, take us by the hand, and keep your hands on us. We pray in Jesus' name. Amen.

Discussion Questions
Lent 3

1. Ask someone to open the session with a prayer.

2. Have a member of the group read Matthew 8:14-17.

3. Having asked them ahead of time, let members of the group share various sections of the chapter.

4. What was the significance of Jesus touching people?

5. What happened to this woman Jesus touched, and what did she do?

6. How has your life been touched by Jesus?

7. What has been the result of it?

8. How have you passed on the touch of Jesus?

9. Let each person offer a prayer, and then close with a benediction by the leader.

Order Of Worship

11:00 a.m.   **Third Sunday In Lent**

WE GATHER TO WORSHIP GOD

Prelude

Chiming the Hour

Introit

Greeting
Leader: In returning and rest you shall be saved;
People: In quietness and in trust shall be your strength.

Hymn of Praise   "To God Be The Glory"

Affirmation of Faith   The Apostles' Creed

Welcome and Sharing

Children's Message   "Give Him Your Hand"

WE TURN TO GOD IN PRAYER

Joys and Concerns

Morning Prayer and the Lord's Prayer

WE GIVE TO GOD

Prayer of Dedication

Offertory

Doxology

44

WE HEAR GOD'S WORD

Hymn of Preparation   "There Is A Balm In Gilead"

Anthem

Reading of the Scriptures   Matthew 8:14-17
Leader: This is the Word of the Lord.
People: Thanks be to God.

The Message   "The Touch Of His Hand"

WE RESPOND TO GOD
The Invitation to Christian Discipleship

Hymn of Invitation   "O Master, Let Me Walk With Thee"

Benediction

Congregational Response

WE DEPART TO SERVE GOD
Postlude

The Treasure Of His Kingdom

Some time ago we had a man speak at one of our suppers who is a shareholder in Mel Fisher's enterprise. Mel Fisher is the man who discovered a Spanish ship which had gone down in a hurricane off the Florida Keys centuries ago. Fisher became fascinated with hunting for lost treasure. Through his research he was able to determine about where the ship went down. He thought it would take him at least twelve weeks to find it. Twelve weeks turned into twelve years, and still there was no treasure. Finally, after sixteen years he discovered the treasure. It is believed to be worth four hundred million dollars.

How would you like to discover some real treasure?

Jesus said the kingdom of Heaven is a treasure. There is no treasure like the treasure of His kingdom.

When Jesus preached the Sermon on the Mount, up near the Galilean city of Capernaum, He made a striking statement about treasure. He said, "Lay not up for yourselves treasures on earth, where moth and rust destroy and where thieves break in and steal; but lay up for yourselves treasure in heaven, where neither moth nor rust destroys and where thieves do not break in and steal. For where your treasure is, there your heart will be also."

Sometime later on Jesus taught again a great multitude of people near that same place. So many came to hear Him that He had to get in a boat and speak to them as they crowded along the shore of the lake. That day He spoke many things to them in parables, those little stories which Jesus told which contained such great truths.

Later, after the people had left, Jesus and the twelve went back to Simon's home in Capernaum. The disciples asked Jesus to explain one of the parables. In the course of their conversation He gave them other parables about the kingdom of Heaven. One of them was the parable I have read for us today. In that parable Jesus

47

said, "The kingdom of heaven is like treasure hidden in a field, which a man found and covered up; then in his joy he goes and sells all that he has and buys that field."

The treasure that man found meant that much to him. But I want to say to all of us today there is no treasure like the treasure of His kingdom.

Jesus came to usher in the new age of God's kingdom. This was one of the great themes of his preaching and teaching. The words "kingdom of heaven" and "kingdom of God" have many meanings. Basically, Jesus was talking about the rule of God in the lives of His people and in the life of the world. It was both present and future, deep within us and all around us.

Jesus said this kingdom is like a treasure hid in a field. It was so valuable a man would sell all his possessions to have it.

Let me tell you these things about the treasure of His kingdom.

I.

First, the treasure of His kingdom creates life's greatest joy. There is simply nothing else which compares with the kingdom of Heaven. In that kingdom is found life's greatest joy. In this parable Jesus told, a man discovered a treasure hidden in a field. Suddenly this man was overwhelmed by joy. It was the greatest discovery he ever made. It filled his life with joy. Jesus was saying the kingdom of Heaven fills our lives with this kind of joy.

The kingdom of Heaven is like this. It creates life's greatest joy.

Everybody wants to find joy. Not everybody is finding it, however. A few years ago there was a song out called, "Looking for love in all the wrong places."

Multitudes of people are looking for happiness in all the wrong places. They would love to be happy, but they cannot define it. They would love to find happiness, but they do not know where it is. They would love to obtain happiness, but they do not know how to go about it. So they are wandering around like sheep without a shepherd.

I understand President Bush wanted to talk to Moses about the situation in the Middle East. So he went up to Heaven and said to

Saint Peter, "Could I possibly see Mr. Moses?" Saint Peter went off to find Moses. In a little while he came back and said, "Moses said the last time he talked to a bush he was lost in the wilderness for forty years." Many people are lost out there looking for happiness.

Sometimes joy, happiness, and fulfillment are seen as being tangible things which we can get, buy, or purchase. We forget so easily that joy never comes to us that way. It is always a byproduct, always the result of something else.

It is found not in the things we possess, but in the things which possess us. It is found not in what we can own, but in who owns us. It is found not in what we create for ourselves, but in what we discover.

C. S. Lewis wrote a book called *Surprised By Joy.* Joy is always a great discovery, a great surprise.

The joy we want is found in our citizenship in God's kingdom, for it is the only place where we really belong. Only there do we find a sense of well-being and fulfillment. Only in God's kingdom do we find an answer for all of life's questions, and a sense of hope for time and eternity. When we make this discovery it begins to fill our lives with joy, a kind of joy which shows up in our living.

A Chinese government official was sent to a village to investigate those who were thought to be Christians. He talked with the village leader about them. He wanted to know how many lived there, and how he could tell who they were. The village leader replied, "That is easy. The Christians are the happy ones."[1]

To discover the treasure of the kingdom of Heaven is to find life's greatest joy.

II.

Second, the treasure of His kingdom costs life's highest price. The greatest joy is never free. It always requires something. The price is high. Jesus said this man in his parable "sells all that he has." He sold everything in order to raise enough money to be able to buy this field in which the treasure was found.

The kingdom of Heaven is like that. It costs life's highest price.

We may look at this negatively. It may seem negative in a way to say the kingdom of Heaven and the Christian life cost us everything. We may feel that makes it seem too difficult, too demanding. Yet, there are so many things like this. There are many things which will cost us everything, and when those things are through with us they will leave us broken and broke.

I saw an interview with Mickey Rooney on television. He said, "I lost $2.00 at a racetrack one time, and I've spent about three million dollars trying to get it back."

Anything we commit our lives to can wind up costing us everything. Everything we choose, every choice we make can cost us everything. That being the case, we have only one sane and sensible choice, and that is to choose the kingdom of God. Yes, it will cost us everything.

A woman in New York earned her living selling pretzels out on the street for 25 cents each. A man came by every day and gave her 25 cents, but he never took a pretzel. He just gave her the money. One day she chased him down and said, "Sir, I need to tell you something about these pretzels." He said, "Oh, I never take one, you know. I just give you the 25 cents." She replied, "Yes, I know. But, they have gone up to 35 cents."

The kingdom of Heaven will always cost us something: everything we are. But as we give everything to it we discover an amazing thing. It begins to take root in us and grow. And it creates within us the very best we can become. It calls forth from us the very best we could ever be. And, like all good investments, it will provide in us and for us wonderful dividends.

A man in one of my churches told me his son came home from Sunday school one Sunday and told his mother they had learned about inheriting God's kingdom. They studied what it means to inherit something. Then he said to his mother, "I'd like my inheritance now." His mother answered, "That's too bad. I'm not through with it yet."

In the kingdom of Heaven, however, you can have your inheritance now. Saint Paul wrote to the Romans, "The Spirit Himself bears witness with our spirit that we are children of God, and if children, then heirs, heirs of God and joint heirs with Christ." In

His final week Jesus told in one of His parables how the king would say, "Come, you blessed of My Father, inherit the kingdom prepared for you from the foundation of the world." It would be given to those who had given their lives in service, to those who had paid the price.

To discover the treasure of the kingdom of Heaven is to learn it costs life's highest price.

III.

Third, the treasure of His kingdom calls for life's deepest commitment. Because the kingdom of Heaven offers us the greatest joy at the highest cost, it calls for the deepest commitment. Jesus tells us that when this man sells all he has in order to raise enough money then he "buys that field." This man made the commitment. He bought it. He followed through with it all the way.

Now, remember the situation here. Jesus has told His disciples this parable about the kingdom of Heaven. He has been training those disciples, and He wants them to be kingdom of God people. He wants them to understand the sacrifice they would be making and the value of that kingdom. He is trying to impress those things upon them.

Christ's kingdom always calls for the note of sacrifice, taking a chance, living on the edge.

There was an Indian down in Florida who used to wrestle alligators for tourists. One time after one of his performances a lady noticed he wore a string of alligator teeth around his neck. She said, "Oh, that is sort of like wearing a string of pearls." He replied, "Not quite. Anyone can open an oyster."

Anyone can be religious. Having kingdom of God treasure is something else altogether. It always requires commitment. It calls us to give our lives to Christ and the rule of God in our lives. It puts us among the people of God who have been faithful to Him across the centuries. It re-orders our priorities, what we think is important, what we are living for. It leads us to dedicate our lives, who we are, what we can do, our abilities, hopes, and dreams to God's kingdom. In the midst of this kind of commitment we make the most marvelous discovery. We find that even though we began thinking it would cost us a great deal, we discover suddenly that we have riches untold, beyond measure. We become overwhelmed by the value of the treasure we have found, the treasure of His kingdom.

There is an ancient legend about some men who were on a long journey. They came across a great desert, and rode into a wilderness area. At sundown they came to a river. They got off their horses and knelt down by the river to drink water. Suddenly a voice spoke to them. The voice said, "Fill your pockets up with pebbles from along the river. And tomorrow you will be both glad and sorry." So they did what the voice commanded. They got on their horses and rode away. On through the night they rode. Finally the sun began to peek over the horizon. They stopped and reached into their pockets and there they found diamonds and rubies. They held a treasure in their hands, and they were both glad and sorry. They were glad they had it, but they were sorry because they had not taken more.[2]

The good news for us is we can have all we want of the treasure of His kingdom, all we are willing to take. If you will take that treasure you will learn it is the discovery of a lifetime.

----

1. Peter Hunt Meek, "An Insufficient Joy," *Pulpit Digest* (Harper & Row Publishers, Inc.: Hagerstown, Maryland, March-April, 1989), p. 62.

2. T. Cecil Myers, *Faith For A Time of Storm* (Abingdon Press: New York and Nashville, 1963), p. 91.

Our Father and our God, who is the giver of all good gifts, we gather to worship Thee and to express our love for Thee for all Thy goodness toward us.

And in this season we think of Thy Son Jesus Christ and the goodness of His life. We thank Thee for the gift of Christ, for His winsome life, His wise teaching, His healing touch, His compassion and mercy, His unselfish death and His victorious resurrection. Enable us to walk through these days with Him.

Help us to open our lives to Him and to be Thy people in all we do.

Give us an unselfish spirit, courage to carry our burdens, the convictions of a great faith and commitment to Thee and Thy kingdom.

Forgive our sins, and enable us to forgive others. Give us patience, and help other people to be patient with us. Make us loving and easy to love. Make us strong, that we may help those who are weak.

Bless the work we do in this church for Thee and Thy kingdom. Help us always to put the welfare of Thy kingdom ahead of our own thoughts, desires, and opinions. Enable us to find the treasure of the kingdom of Christ.

Bless our sick and sorrowful, and those in our community who need Thy help and ours. Bless suffering people the world over.

Bless the leaders of the world, O God, with wisdom, compassion, and good sense. We pray these things in the name of Thy well-beloved Son. Amen.

Finding Buried Treasure

Good morning, boys and girls. I am so glad you have come to church today.

I have brought with me today a little shovel for us to look at. Now, this has many good uses. You could dig a hole for a fence post. Or you could dig a ditch to drain away water. You could use it to prepare the ground for a flower bed or a small garden. Can any of you think of any other ways to use this shovel?

You could also use it to dig for buried treasure. Maybe some of you have read a popular book called *Treasure Island*. It's a book about pirates and buried treasure.

One time Jesus was talking to some people. We are going to read about this later on today. He told a story about a man who found a treasure buried in a field. That man sold everything he had so he could have enough money to buy the field. Jesus was saying that to love God and live for God is that important. It is worth that much.

Jesus used a term, "the Kingdom of God." By that He meant God's rule in our lives. It is letting God be our ruler, the one we love and serve and obey. It is giving our lives to God.

For us to do this is more valuable to us than any treasure we could ever find. It is the most important thing we could ever have or discover. The most important decision we ever make is deciding to make God our king and then living in His kingdom.

So, don't let this treasure stay buried. Dig it up. Open it up and live on it.

Let's bow our heads. O God, thank You for the gift of your Son for the treasure we find in Him and You. Amen.

Discussion Questions
Lent 4

1. Begin the session with a prayer by a group member.

2. Have someone read Matthew 13:44.

3. Having asked them ahead of time, let members of the group share various sections of the chapter.

4. What is Jesus saying in this parable?

5. Why did He think the Kingdom of God was so valuable?

6. How valuable is the Kingdom of God to you?

7. Why is this so?

8. If the Kingdom of God is so valuable to you, what then will you do about it?

9. Close with a time of silent prayer, sentence prayers, and then the benediction by the leader.

Order Of Worship

11:00 a.m.   **Fourth Sunday In Lent**

WE GATHER TO WORSHIP GOD
Prelude

Chiming the Hour

Introit

Greeting
Leader: Rend your hearts and not your clothing.
People: Return to the Lord, your God, for He is gracious and merciful.

Hymn of Praise   "O Worship The King"

Affirmation of Faith   The Apostles' Creed

Welcome and Sharing

Children's Message   "Finding Buried Treasure"

WE TURN TO GOD IN PRAYER
Joys and Concerns

Morning Prayer and the Lord's Prayer

WE GIVE TO GOD
Prayer of Dedication

Offertory

Doxology

WE HEAR GOD'S WORD

Hymn of Preparation   "I Love Thy Kingdom, Lord"

Anthem

Reading of the Scriptures   Matthew 13:44
Leader: This is the Word of the Lord.
People: Thanks be to God.

The Message   "The Treasure Of His Kingdom"

WE RESPOND TO GOD
The Invitation to Christian Discipleship

Hymn of Invitation   "Jesus, Keep Me Near The Cross"

Benediction

Congregational Response

WE DEPART TO SERVE GOD
Postlude

The Test Of His Courage

A man and his wife had their vacation interrupted by a terrible toothache. They knew no one in the little town by the interstate highway. But they drove into town and asked for directions to the nearest dentist. They went straight to the dentist's office and told the receptionist they had an emergency situation. They had to see the dentist immediately. The receptionist showed them into a little room, and in a minute the dentist came in. They stood up to greet him, and the wife said, "We are on a trip and we have a tooth that must come out. We have no time for any shots or gas, but it has to come out right now. Just pull it out now." The dentist agreed to pull the tooth the old-fashioned way, and said, "Which tooth is it?" The woman turned to her husband and said, "Show him your tooth, dear."

How much courage do you really have?

Years ago the great theologian Paul Tillich wrote a book called *The Courage To Be*. In that book he said, "The courage to be is the ethical act in which man affirms his own being in spite of those elements of his existence which conflict with his essential self-affirmation."[1]

Courage means we know who we are in spite of everything which seems to be against us, and because of our courage we can face even those things which threaten to destroy us.

Jesus was a man of courage because He was willing to go up to Jerusalem and face the things which were waiting on Him there. There were people and forces waiting there to destroy Him. This was to be a real test of His courage.

Several times Jesus talked with His disciples about going to Jerusalem. It seems the closer they got to it, the more He talked with them about it, naturally so. Late in Matthew's gospel we find Jesus and the twelve getting ready to go there.

In chapter seventeen Matthew tells us, "As they were gathering in Galilee, Jesus said to them, 'The Son of man is to be delivered into the hands of men, and they will kill him, and he will be raised on the third day.' And they were greatly distressed."

Three chapters later Matthew writes, "Then Jesus, going up to Jerusalem, took the twelve disciples aside on the road and said to them, 'Behold, we are going up to Jerusalem; and the Son of man will be delivered to the chief priests and scribes, and they will condemn him to death, and deliver him to the Gentiles to be mocked and scourged and crucified, and he will be raised on the third day.' "

Jesus was about to face the real test of His courage. But strangely enough these are the moments for which He was born. These are the moments for which He had been living. These are the moments which threatened to break Him, but they are really the moments which would make Him. Because of that Jesus was willing to face Jerusalem, knowing He was carrying out His Father's good will and His Father would see Him through. In that He found His courage.

So, let me suggest some things about His experience which will speak to our own experience, and our need of this kind of courage. First, hang on to this.

I.

When there is no way out — let God in. Sometimes there is no way out. Jesus knew it was true. There was no way to avoid going up to Jerusalem. So He told His disciples they were going there, "and the Son of Man will be delivered into the hands of the chief priests, and the scribes, and they will condemn Him to death." There was no way out.

Jesus did not come to this realization out there on the road, and He did not decide to let God in at that time. He made this decision way back up there before He even left Nazareth. He made it there at the Jordan River when He was baptized and heard the voice of God saying, "This is my Son in whom I am well pleased." He made it when He went back to Nazareth to preach at the beginning of His ministry and read those words, "The Spirit of the Lord is upon me because He has anointed me to preach the gospel...." When He sat down He said, "Today this scripture is fulfilled in your hearing."

Jesus knew there was no way out, and He let God in. He made the presence of God, serving God, obeying God the center of His life. Everything else was seen against the background of God's rule in His life.

Sometimes we face things we would like to get out of, not have to face. We all have those difficult moments. We discover many times there is no way out.

I heard about a marriage made in Heaven. This couple was to be married late in life, but before the wedding they died in a traffic accident. When they got to Heaven they asked Saint Peter if they could still get married. He said, "Let me see what I can do." They waited for about a year. Finally, he told them everything had been arranged. But, they said, "Look, we have been thinking. What if this does not work? Can we get a divorce and get out of this marriage?" He said, "What do you mean? Don't even talk to me about that. Why, it took me a year to find a preacher up here!"

There are times when we face situations for which there is no way out. When there is no way out, then we must prepare ourselves to face what is before us.

A young man was flunking out of college. He sent a telegram to his mother, "Flunked out. Prepare Dad." He received an answer right back, "Dad prepared. Prepare yourself."

How do we prepare for the things for which there is no way out? There is only one thing to do. Let God in. If we will let God in, then all the things we do will be against the background of God's rule in our lives. Whatever happens to us, we will know that God is in control of the situation and us.

A lady was shopping at the grocery store one afternoon. She suddenly became aware that her little girl was not with her. She walked over a few aisles and saw her with several other ladies, and heard her calling, "Marjorie!" She said, "Here I am. Why didn't you call 'Mama'?" The girl answered, "I tried that. You'd be surprised how many mommies came. But when I called for 'Marjorie' I knew you'd be here."[2]

Jesus knew He could call on His Father, and so can we. When there is no way out, let God in. Then, hang on to this.

II.

When there is no way around — follow God through. Sometimes there is no way around. Jesus knew it was true. There was no way around Jerusalem. The road He was on led there. He had to go there and face His enemies and the cross. So He told His disciples as they walked that road that He would be delivered "into the hands of the Gentiles to mock and to scourge." There was no way around that.

Later we see Him there in the garden as He prays, "Father, if you are willing let this cup pass from me; nevertheless, not my will but Thine be done." Jesus knew there was no way around, and He decided to follow God through, to face what was before Him. He did not make that decision there in the garden. He did not make it on the road to Jerusalem. He made it much earlier than that.

Sometimes we face things we would like to avoid, to go around, not have to confront. And many times we discover there is no way around.

A boy went off to camp, though he did not really want to go. After a few days he wrote a letter home. It said, "Dear Mom and Dad, I told you something terrible would happen if I went off to camp. Well, it did. Love, Joe."[3]

Another boy went on a skiing trip with the youth of his church. He sent home a card which said, "Yesterday we learned how to ski. I'm not very good. I broke a leg. Thank goodness it wasn't mine."[4]

Some things we cannot avoid. When there is no way around, then we must prepare ourselves to confront what is before us. How do we do that?

There is only one way. Follow God through. If we will follow God through, then we will be able to find our way with our hands in God's hands. And He will lead us in His ways.

In the midst of battle a young man became afraid. He knew there was a great possibility that he would not make it. He decided to run. The pressure was too much. But when he turned around, there stood his general. He said to the young man, "Your road lies that way."[5] It always does.

Jesus knew He had to stay on the road, but on the road He would be following God. When there is no way around, follow God through. Finally, hang onto this.

III.

When there is no way off — go with God over. Sometimes there is no way off. Jesus knew it was true. There was no way for Him to get off. So He told His disciples they would "crucify Him." There was no way off, no way to get off from this. But then He added, "The third day He will rise again." Jesus knew there was no way off the cross, but there was a way over the cross. The New Testament calls it resurrection.

Because of this Jesus could promise His disciples on the night before the cross, "In the world you have tribulation: But be of good cheer; I have overcome the world."

Sometimes we face things we would like to get off from, not have to bear, not have to endure. Many times we discover we cannot find an easy way off. When there is no way off, we must prepare to endure what is facing us.

How do we prepare for the things from which there is no way off? There is only one thing to do. Go with God over. So many people have been able to do that.

Maybe you think you are facing something you cannot handle, something overwhelming which is greater than you are. Maybe you feel you have a cross too great to bear. When there is no way off, go with God over.

Alan Walker told about a young preacher who went to be the pastor of a small church. During his first year he developed two great goals. One was to build a new church, and the other was to marry a girl in the choir. He reached both of those goals in his second year there. But during the third year the new building burned down, and then his wife died in a tragic accident. This experience nearly destroyed him. One day he went out for a walk and went into a church. He went in and sat down. While he was there something wonderful happened to him. He said later of that experience, "When I went in, all the stars had gone out of my sky. When I came back out, God had lit them again."[6]

Jesus knew what that final week in Jerusalem would mean. He knew that for all of those who loved Him the stars would be torn out of their sky. Those people and those forces in Jerusalem were waiting to do Him in, and there was no way off for Jesus. They would hang Jesus on a cross. But they did not know that God was putting Him there, and they did not know that Jesus had the courage to face it, saying, "If I be lifted up I will draw all men unto me." He knew out of that terrible experience waiting on Him would come the dawn of a new day. In that He found His courage.

The things which threatened to break Jesus are the things which would make Jesus. His life, His victory is a promise for all of us.

So when there is no way out, let God in. When there is no way around, follow God through. When there is no way off, go with God over. "In the world you have tribulation; But be of good cheer; I have overcome the world."

---

1. Paul Tillich, *The Courage To Be* (Yale University Press: New Haven and London, 1952), p. 3.

2. Bruce Larson, *The Presence* (Harper & Row Publishers: San Francisco, 1988), p. 22.

3. Brian L. Harbour, "Super Single Or Dynamic Duo?" *Award Winning Sermons,* Volume I (Broadman Press: Nashville, 1977), p. 29.

4. Ernest A. Fitzgerald, *You Can Believe* (Abingdon Press: Nashville and New York, 1975), p. 30.

5. Wallace Chappell, *The Trumpet's Certain Sound* (Wallace Chappell Ministries, Inc.: Nashville, 1987), p. 27.

6. Alan Walker, *God, The Disturber* (Word Books: Waco, Texas, 1973), p. 27.

Eternal God and Father of us all, who has shown Thyself to us in the coming of Thy Son, we have gathered here in His name to worship Thee and to thank Thee for all Thy bountiful gifts upon us. For the greatest gift, the gift of Thy Son, we thank Thee, O God. And as we thank Thee for His wonderful birth, His unselfish life, His marvelous deeds, His transforming words, and His precious death, prepare us to celebrate soon His triumphant resurrection.

May we continue in these days of Lent to follow faithfully along with Him as He heads toward that awful place where Heaven and Hell collided. Give us the kind of courage He had. Keep us near the cross and an empty tomb.

Continue, gracious God, to give us the things we need for living. Give us a strong faith. Put a new song in our hearts. Make us to be people of hope. Help us to put Thee, Thy Son, and Thy kingdom first in our lives so that we would give ourselves to Thee and never count the cost, or fall short, or give up, or quit believing, or fail to dream. Make our dreams for Thee come true.

Continue to bless the witness of this church. Bless the ways we serve Thee and the people of our own community and even to the ends of the earth. Enable us to touch the lives of others for Christ across the street and across the world.

Bless with Thy hands of mercy people of our church and community who need Thy touch in whatever way, whether it is in sickness, sorrow, pain, loneliness, or a lack of nerve.

Give us enough nerve to serve Thee and the needs of hurting people, and we will strive to serve Thee and please Thee in all we do, for we pray in His holy name. Amen.

Can You Pass The Test?

I want to welcome you to our service today. I am really glad you are here with us for worship this Sunday. We are moving right along in the season of Lent. Today is the fifth Sunday in Lent. Next Sunday is what we call Palm Sunday, and the next Sunday is Easter Sunday.

On these Sundays we have been thinking together about Jesus going to Jerusalem. Today we come closer to that time. I want us to think today about how brave Jesus was during those days.

Now, I am going to pass out to each of you a piece of paper and a pen. Then I will call out some words to you. You write them down. Here are the words: cat, house, run, boat. What have we just done? That's right. This was a spelling test. I bet you have one every week in school. When I was your age we had one every Friday. It was important to study and to be able to pass the test. You have tests you must pass all the way through school.

There are other times when we have tests. It is not just in school. Life has many tests for us. Sometimes these are difficult things we go through which test our courage, or how brave or how strong we are.

Jesus had a time when He was tested. This was a test of His courage. But He passed the test. He was brave enough to go to Jerusalem and face His enemies. And He promised His disciples He would always be with them.

And do you know what? He is always with us to help us. Because He is, we can face all the things which test us and we can pass the tests we face.

May we pray. O God, make us to be strong and make us brave, just like your Son and our Friend Jesus was always brave, for we know He is with us. Amen.

Discussion Questions
Lent 5

1. Begin with a prayer by a group member.

2. Have someone read Matthew 20:17-19.

3. Having asked them ahead of time, let members of the group share various sections of the chapter.

4. What was it that brought Jesus to this point?

5. What was at stake here during this time?

6. Did the Disciples understand what was happening?

7. How do you respond to such situations in your own life?

8. What is it that sees you through such times?

9. Close with sentence prayers and a benediction.

Order Of Worship

11:00 a.m.   **Fifth Sunday In Lent**

WE GATHER TO WORSHIP GOD

Prelude

Chiming the Hour

Introit

Greeting
Leader: What shall I render to the Lord for all his bounty to me?
**People: I will lift up the cup of salvation and call on the name
        of the Lord.**

Hymn of Praise   "Come, Christians, Join To Sing"

Affirmation of Faith   The Apostles' Creed

Welcome and Sharing

Children's Message   "Can You Pass The Test?"

WE TURN TO GOD IN PRAYER

Joys and Concerns

Morning Prayer and the Lord's Prayer

WE GIVE TO GOD

Prayer of Dedication

Offertory

Doxology

WE HEAR GOD'S WORD

Hymn of Preparation "Beneath The Cross Of Jesus"

Anthem

Reading of the Scriptures Matthew 20:17-19
Leader: This is the Word of the Lord.
People: Thanks be to God.

The Message "The Test Of His Courage"

WE RESPOND TO GOD

The Invitation to Christian Discipleship

Hymn of Invitation "O Jesus, I Have Promised"

Benediction

Congregational Response

WE DEPART TO SERVE GOD

Postlude

Palm Sunday
Matthew 21:1-10

The Tragedy Of His Victory

Some of you experienced the victory of World War II. Others of us have at least seen on television old newsreel footage of the celebration of victory in Europe. Then came victory over Japan and other victory parades. There were no such celebrations after the wars in Korea and Vietnam. But after the Allied victory in the Persian Gulf we attempted to make up for all of that with tremendous celebrations and victory parades. The attention of the entire nation was fixed on General Norman Schwarzkopf, who was the man of the hour.

It is an ancient custom dating back in history to other times and other places, where kings and warriors were welcomed home with victory celebrations and parades through city gates.

It happened in Jerusalem whenever a new king ascended the throne. The people turned out and lined the streets. They spread their garments on the ground and waved palm branches in the air shouting, "Hosanna! Blessed is he who comes in the name of the Lord."

Then one day long after the Israelite kings had gone and there was no more glory and nothing to celebrate, Jesus came. "Who is this?" the people in the street asked. Some of them answered, "This is Jesus, the prophet from Nazareth of Galilee."

He had come to Jerusalem from Galilee, down the Jordan Valley, through the streets of Jericho, up that long, winding road toward the city of Jerusalem. He and His disciples stopped out there at a little village called Bethphage, just before the Mount of Olives. Jesus sent two disciples into the village to get a donkey. Then Jesus got on that donkey and rode over the Mount of Olives, heading toward the gate of the city of Jerusalem.

How did He know the donkey would be there? Someone left it for Him. How did the people know He was coming to the city?

71

Someone let them know. How did they know it was Jesus, the man from Galilee, the one rumored to be the new king of the Jews? Someone told them who He was, "This is Jesus, the prophet from Nazareth of Galilee."

The man from Galilee had finally come. Now He faced Jerusalem. And all these people turned out to see Him, to give Him a victory parade. V-J Day, Victory in Jerusalem, had finally come. "Hosanna to the Son of David! Blessed is He who comes in the name of the Lord! Hosanna in the highest!" But there was something wrong there. It was a hollow victory. There was an undercurrent moving through the crowd, in the minds of the disciples, into the heart of Jesus. Jerusalem was nothing like Galilee. There was a tension in the air.

This is not a real victory of any lasting duration. There is a great veil of tragedy which falls over this episode. It is a tragic kind of victory.

Today Palm Sunday is a reminder of this fact. Palm Sunday always stands as a great divider. It separates us into two groups of people who either simply have opinions about what a nice fellow Jesus must have been, or who dare to cast our lots with Him. It separates us into either those who follow public opinion and go along with the crowd, or those who are willing to leave the safety of the crowd and walk through the gates of the city with Him.

I would remind you that some of these who are shouting, "Hosanna to the Son of David," on Palm Sunday will be shouting, "Give us Barabbas!" when Friday comes.

The tragedy of Palm Sunday always confronts us with a choice. As we think about Jesus going to Jerusalem and the people who greeted Him, remember this.

I.

The tragedy was their participation was nearly void. It was void of any real sincerity. Many of those people just turned out to watch Jesus go by. We know from the Gospels, as Matthew tells us, that "Most of the crowd spread their garments on the road." But what were these people doing? Did they really know? Did they really care who this person was and what He was all about?

There must have been many people in Jerusalem who were loyal followers of Jesus. It is true that by this time many people had fallen away from Him. But there were many who were still with Him. For so many in Jerusalem on that day, however, there must have been little meaning in what was going on. Their participation was void of any real commitment to Jesus and who He was, what He was all about, and what His entry into Jerusalem really meant. Many of those people had long ago lost the meaning of who they were and the spirit of their faith.

A woman was cleaning out her canary's cage when the phone rang. With the vacuum cleaner in one hand she answered the phone with the other, and before she could turn off the vacuum cleaner her little bird was gone. She told her friend she would call her right back. She pulled the bird out of the machine, washed him off in the sink, blow dried him, and set him back on his perch. When she talked with her friend she said, "I think he will be all right. But he just sits there with a funny look on his face, staring straight ahead, not singing anymore."

Jerusalem had been through the mill many times. And many of those people in Jerusalem must have been void of any real feeling.

One of the reasons they reacted to Jesus the way they did was that they could not accept the things He had been saying. They were looking for a new king who would free them from Rome. They wanted that kind of kingdom and its glory. But the kingdom talk they had heard from Jesus had to do with God's kingdom, a kingdom within them, a kingdom which had already come.

E. Stanley Jones, the great missionary, tells of being in South Africa on a preaching mission. The pastor who traveled with him said, "You preach a troublesome gospel. We preach a kingdom in heaven hereafter that upsets nothing now. But you preach a kingdom now on earth and that upsets everything."[1]

The preaching of Jesus upset everything because He preached that the kingdom of God is here all around us, within us, God ruling in our lives. On this Palm Sunday would you be willing to let that kingdom live in you? And would you be willing to participate in what that kingdom means?

73

II.

Then remember this also. The tragedy was that their exaltation was merely verbal. They gave Jesus lip service on that first Palm Sunday. Many of them cried out, "Hosanna to the Son of David! Blessed is He who comes in the name of the Lord! Hosanna in the highest!" They gave Jesus lip service, and that is all many of them gave Him. Their exaltation was merely a verbal exercise.

Oh, they were willing to join in the chorus as long as it cost nothing. After all, there was no real risk in standing by the road watching the parade go by. But the call of Jesus had always meant more than that. It had always required the complete giving of a person's life to Him and what He was all about.

The truth is Jesus did not need that kind of exaltation. He did not require or want this kind of lip service. He did not try to stop it. But apparently the Pharisees did. Luke, in his version of the story, tells us that when the Pharisees saw what was happening and heard the shouts, "Blessed is the king who comes in the name of the Lord," they said to Jesus, "Teacher, rebuke your disciples." Jesus replied to them, "I tell you if these should keep silent, the stones would immediately cry out." Jesus accepted what was being shouted and many were sincere in this, but for most of them their exaltation was merely verbal.

A few years ago a man and his wife came out of church and spoke to me. I knew they had been away on a month-long trip, and I asked them how it went. He said, "It was fine. And while we were gone we did not hear a preacher anywhere as good as you are." I straightened up a bit and was trying to think of some response when he said, "We didn't hear any preacher at all. We didn't go to church."

Just so many in Jerusalem were saying to Jesus, "We never heard anyone like you." Jesus had no trouble drawing a crowd. But it was not verbal support that He needed.

Still today it is not verbal support that Jesus needs. No, still today He needs men and women, young people and children who will step out of the crowd on the side of the road and walk with Him. That is the call of Jesus, to come follow Him, not just to cheer as He walks by alone. Always it means the commitment of a life to Him, something more than just lip service, something beyond a merely verbal exaltation.

74

A man had become very successful and was invited to come back to speak in the little church in the town where he had grown up. He told about many of his childhood experiences. He said that once he heard a preacher say we should give all we have to Jesus. Then he said, "As a boy I heard that statement and decided I would. I had $1.82, and I gave it all to Jesus. That has made a big difference in my life, and has caused me to be blessed. As you know, I now own a large company. Thousands work for me. I don't know what I'm worth, but it's a lot." He paused a moment and a little boy said, "Mister, would you do it again? Would you give all you have to Jesus now?"

On this Palm Sunday are you willing to give Jesus something other than just a good word? Would you give Him your life and join Him on the road?

III.

Finally, remember this. The tragedy was that their recognition was clearly visual. It was nothing more than that for so many of them. Matthew tells us that "All the city was stirred, saying, 'Who is this?' " So the multitude replied, "This is the prophet Jesus from Nazareth of Galilee." They recognized Him. But it was only a visual kind of recognition. They were not really recognizing Him as the ruler of their lives.

However, this is the call of Palm Sunday. That is the challenge Palm Sunday always causes us to face. This is true because the time comes when we simply have to choose.

As the week went on, the wave of popular approval died down. More and more Jesus was alone as less and less people supported Him. Finally, in the end He stands alone.

So, today we face a choice. It is the call to recognize Him for who He is, and to do that by making Him the ruler of our lives.

One Palm Sunday at Riverside Church in New York, Harry Emerson Fosdick preached a sermon called "An Unavoidable Choice Faces Our Jerusalem, Too."[2]

It is a choice we always face. Today on Palm Sunday that choice is before us. There are many ways we can make that choice by giving ourselves to Him and serving Him through His church. To recognize who He is compels us to serve Him.

In one of our great cities a minister served in a ghetto community. Once while talking with a friend he told him about his work, all the human suffering he saw, and how hard it was for him to face it every day. His friend said to him, "Why don't you just run away from it all?" He replied, "I would do just that, but a strange man on a cross won't let me."

Maybe there are times when some of us are tempted to take the easy way and live only for ourselves, with no concern about the hurts of the world, the challenge of Christ, the call of the church, the demands of the kingdom. But that strange man on a cross who went to face Jerusalem will not let us get away, or get off so easily, or disappear into some safe harbor of escapism. Always He calls us to meet Him in the road and go with Him.

Hugh Latimer was a great preacher in England. Once while he was preaching at Westminster Abbey he saw the King of England in the congregation. Hugh Latimer said, "Latimer! Latimer! Latimer! Be careful what you say. The King of England is here!" He paused a moment and then he said, "Latimer! Latimer! Latimer! Be careful what you say. The King of kings is here."[3]

Palm Sunday confronts us with this truth. The King of kings is here facing us in our own Jerusalem. He calls us never to be careful again, to be willing to give up safety and approval, to give up ease and escapism, to step out into the street and follow Him to the end — and the beginning.

"Hosanna to the Son of David! Blessed is He who comes in the name of the Lord! Hosanna in the highest!"

Who is this Jesus? This is the prophet from Nazareth of Galilee.

Would you go with Him? Would you dare?

---

1. E. Stanley Jones, *The Unshakable Kingdom and The Unchanging Person* (Abingdon Press: Nashville and New York, 1972), p. 69.

2. Harry Emerson Fosdick, *On Being Fit To Live With* (Harper & Brothers: New York and London, 1946), p. 203.

3. William Barclay, *The Gospel of Luke* (The Westminster Press: Philadelphia, 1953), p. 192.

Morning Prayer
Palm Sunday

O God, as we gather here on this Palm Sunday we lift our voices as in days of old, "Hosanna in the highest! Blessed is He that cometh in the name of the Lord!" Enable us to open our lives to Him so that He would be able to come in and be the king of our lives.

Help us this week to watch and pray with our Lord. Enable us to remember His passion and to identify ourselves with Him, for in His passion He identified Himself with us and took upon Himself all the hurt, sorrow, pain, sin, and suffering that is a part of our lives. May we walk with Him down crowded streets, in lonely places, through deep valleys, and up hills of struggle.

We thank Thee today, O God, for the coming of Thy Son into the world and all He has done for us and for all the world. And we thank Thee for all Thy blessings upon us, for out of Thy hands of goodness and mercy every good thing has come to us. Accept our thanksgiving, gracious God.

Continue to make Thy ways known to us. Make Thy paths straight and help us to walk in them. Continue to be for us a light that shines in the darkness so that we would find our way into Thy will and good purposes for our living.

Strengthen our faith, confirm our hope, perfect us in love. Fill our lives with grace. Make us to be people of compassion and mercy. Forgive our sins. Mold us into the image of Thy Son.

Touch the lives of those among us who are sick, and those in sorrow, and those who struggle under great burdens.

Help people the world over who need Thy help, and do this through our hands, as much as we can. We pray these things in the name of Thy Son. Amen.

Welcome The King

Today is Palm Sunday, and this is a special day for us. I want to welcome you to our service today. I am so glad you are here. Make yourself at home. If you need anything, you let me know.

Now, you see, I have tried to welcome you today. And this is what Palm Sunday is all about. When Jesus went to the city of Jerusalem, all the people turned out to see Him and to welcome Him.

They did not welcome Him like they would any other person, for there was something different about Him and about that day. They welcomed Him as the new king of the Jews. For hundreds of years they had welcomed a new king into the city with shouts of "Hosanna!" But it had been a long time since they had been able to do that, for they had been ruled by other countries. There had been no king there for centuries, except they now had old King Herod, a mean king who worked for the Romans, really. There had been another King Herod earlier. But these kings were not like the good kings who had ruled. So the people were waiting for a good king to come and help them. Many people thought Jesus was that king, and that He would defeat the Romans and make them leave.

However, Jesus came to set up the Kingdom of God, a kingdom which is in our hearts. He came to be our King still today. Palm Sunday reminds us of this. You can welcome this king into your heart.

We do that by learning about Him, worshiping Him, serving Him, loving Him, and trying to live like Him. We let him be our king still today. I hope all of us will do just that.

Now, may we bow our heads as we pray. O God, help us to open our hearts and let our king Jesus come in. Amen.

1. Begin with a prayer led by a group member.

2. Have someone read Matthew 21:1-10.

3. Having asked them ahead of time, let members of the group share various sections of the chapter.

4. What forces awaited Jesus as He entered Jerusalem?

5. How was He able to face them?

6. What things in life oppose you?

7. How is it that you overcome them?

8. What does your struggle really mean?

9. Have someone read Psalm 22. Then, share sentence prayers and a benediction.

Order Of Worship

Palm Sunday

WE GATHER TO WORSHIP GOD
Prelude

Chiming the Hour

Introit

Greeting
Leader: Hosanna to the Son of David! Hosanna in the highest!
People: Blessed is the one who comes in the name of the Lord.

Hymn of Praise   "Hosanna, Loud Hosanna"

Affirmation of Faith   The Apostles' Creed

Welcome and Sharing

Children's Message   "Welcome The King"

WE TURN TO GOD IN PRAYER
Joys and Concerns

Morning Prayer and the Lord's Prayer

WE GIVE TO GOD
Prayer of Dedication

Offertory

Doxology

81

WE HEAR GOD'S WORD

Hymn of Preparation   "Tell Me The Stories Of Jesus"

Anthem

Reading of the Scriptures   Matthew 21:1-10
Leader: This is the Word of the Lord.
People: Thanks be to God.

The Message   "The Tragedy Of His Victory"

WE RESPOND TO GOD

The Invitation to Christian Discipleship

Hymn of Invitation   "Lead On, O King Eternal"

Benediction

Congregational Response

WE DEPART TO SERVE GOD

Postlude

The Triumph Of His Defeat

Bishop Walter L. Underwood wrote a book a few years ago called *Being Human Being Hopeful*. The last chapter is on the subject of death. He refers to a statement made by actor Woody Allen, who said, "I don't want immortality through my work. I want immortality through not dying."[1] I read that book with great interest. Then I learned that Bishop Underwood died not long after I had read his book, and I went back and read that last chapter again. It is a great affirmation of our faith in the face of life's greatest question.

When Christian missionaries landed on the island we now call England, they were taken to see the king of Northhumbria. The missionaries told of their Christian faith. When they were through with what they had to say, someone asked, "Can this new religion tell us anything of what happens after death?"[2] That is always the question.

When Bishop Earl G. Hunt was serving as a college president, he and his wife entertained Lord Caradon, the British Ambassador to the United Nations. He was delivering a lecture on their campus. One evening during dinner he asked about the hymns which were sung in the South. He said, "Do you ever sing "Beulah Land'?" He then told what the words of that hymn had meant to him and how it had helped him so many times.[3]

The resurrection of our Lord and Savior Jesus Christ is God's answer for all our questions, fears, and doubts. It is the assurance of all our hopes, dreams, and desires.

The resurrection of Christ is the great watershed of history. It is the all-time most important event ever to take place in this world. All our hopes and dreams are centered in this. All our sorrows and heartaches find their relief in this.

This is the day of God's triumph. It is the day God defeated the power of sin and death. It is the day God took a stand and said, "That is enough."

They took His Son out and lashed Him with a whip. They mocked Him and insulted Him. They pressed down hard a crown of thorns. They led Him through the streets, a public spectacle. They took Him to a place outside the walls of the city, and there they nailed Him to a cross. Then they left Him there for dead.

God said, "That is enough. I will not stand for any more of this." That day ended with God biding His time. The next day came, a silent Saturday, and still God said nothing and did nothing. Then the first day of the week began to dawn. Now God was ready. Now He would do something about all this. Now He would take a stand and take a hand in what had been done to His boy.

On that day a new dawn broke upon the face of the earth. With the dawn of that new day the women made their way out to a garden tomb. There they made a world-shaking, history-making, breathtaking discovery which transformed their lives and the lives of all of His followers from that moment to this: "Christ the Lord is risen today."

Nothing has ever been the same. They thought they had defeated Jesus, but out of that defeat had come triumph, glory, resurrection. Today on this glorious Easter Sunday think back over the events of that day when God brought triumph out of defeat. Here are the facts.

I.

They defeated Jesus and sent Him to the tomb — but He overcame the power of death. God raised Him up. The tomb could not hold Him. As the women went out to that tomb in a garden there was an earthquake. The angel of the Lord came down and rolled away the stone. Then the angel said to the women, "Do not be afraid, for I know that you seek Jesus who was crucified. He is not here; for He is risen, as He said. Come, see the place where the Lord lay."

The power of death had no power over Him, for the power of death was made weak by the power of God. The tomb could not hold Him, for God was greater than the tomb, and the bonds of God's love were stronger than the bonds of that tomb. The enemies of Jesus could not keep Him, for God defeated all of His enemies.

The dawn brought the sunrise of a new day, a new age, a new reality. That new reality, the reality of resurrection, transforms everything. Everything can now be seen from the standpoint of the new reality of the resurrection of Christ who went before us and found a new way.

A little boy at camp one summer listened intently as the lifeguard instructed all the campers in rules for safe swimming. He told them about the importance of each person having a buddy. After he finished he blew his whistle and said, "Okay, now. Tell me, what does it mean to have a buddy?" The little boy replied, "A buddy is someone who drowns with you."

Jesus was willing to die with us, and then to bring into our experience the new reality of resurrection. This new reality touches all of life. It is our hope for today and tomorrow for our loved ones and for ourselves. It is the promise of victory over death. It is also a new element which comes into our living. The power of the resurrection is not only what we believe in for the future, it is also what we live by in the present. Saint Paul writes to the Romans in chapter six that "just as Christ was raised from the dead by the glory of the Father, even so we also should walk in newness of life."

The resurrection becomes a power at work in our lives. Even in the face of all that would defeat us, all the suffering we go through, all the situations we think are hopeless, in all of that we find in the resurrection of Christ the power, the hope, the strength to go on. Because He overcame the power of death, nothing is ever the same.

At the Grand Canyon on Easter Sunday a sunrise service is held each year. During that service a great stone is rolled over the edge and it goes bouncing down the side of the canyon while someone reads this passage from Matthew about the stone being rolled away. Then a choir sings, "King of kings and Lord of lords."[4]

He overcame the power of death.

II.

Second, they defeated Jesus and all who loved Him mourned — but He said to them, "Rejoice!" It was a complete turnaround. For two days they had been in mourning. The women went out there to anoint His body with spices. But a time of mourning was turned into a time of rejoicing.

Easter means this still today. Our times of mourning can be transformed, and even in the midst of them we may find a way through. There are many times for all of us when life gets bogged down in sorrows and heartaches, when it seems to be going nowhere and nothing good is happening.

A man was fishing in a farmer's pond. The farmer came out and caught him. He said to the man, "Do you see that sign? It says 'No Fishing.' " The man looked at the sign, and said to the farmer, "Whoever painted that sign knew what he was talking about."

There are so many times when life seems empty, when it seems we may lose our way, when there is no fishing.

Not long after the resurrection the disciples went back up to Galilee. Simon Peter said, "I am going fishing." The other disciples went with him. They fished all night and there was no fishing. They caught nothing. Early that next morning Jesus stood on the shore and called out to them, "Children, have you any food?" When they responded negatively, Jesus replied, "Cast the net on the right side of the boat, and you will find food."

There are times when in spite of Easter we keep looking on the wrong side, the empty side. In those times there is no fishing.

A taxi driver picked up a lady at a hospital in Chicago. He noticed her weeping, and after a few minutes began talking with her. He found out her mother had died. Then he asked her if she and her mother were Christians. When the woman said yes, he said, "Then why are you crying as if everything was over?"[5]

Everything is never over because of the resurrection of Jesus Christ, and the operative word in the midst of our sorrows and suffering is always "Rejoice!"

III.

Third, they defeated Jesus and put an end to what He began — but He assured them there was no end. A new beginning grew out of what was thought to be a tragic ending. Jesus said to the women, "Do not be afraid. Go and tell my brethren to go to Galilee, and there they will see me." It was not the end at all. No one could put an end to what Jesus had begun. He had lit a fire in the hearts of His disciples which would never go out, a light shining in the darkness.

He had told them early, way back up there in Galilee on the side of a mountain, "You are the light of the world ... Let your light so shine before men...." It was the light of the resurrection, a light which no darkness has ever or will ever put out. The message of Easter is still that same message: "Do not be afraid. Go and tell my brothers and sisters they will see me. I will meet them." He will always meet us out there in the future.

In every situation, every challenge, every sorrow, He will meet us.

In every act of kindness, mercy, and compassion, He will meet us and be with us.

In every kind of ministry, service, and witness, He will meet us and bless what we do, give, and hope.

In every time of study, prayer, and worship, He will meet us and be in the midst of us.

Some of you saw a movie a few years ago called *Places In The Heart.* It is the story of a heroic woman, played by Sally Fields, whose husband is killed in the line of duty as a sheriff in a small town. Somehow she survives this tragedy, and manages to earn a living for her family on their farm. During the story a black man who works for her is beaten by a mob and has to leave. But with the closing scene you suddenly become aware that something is different. Here they all are in church receiving the Lord's Supper together: her husband, his killer, her former employee.

I remember the feeling I had when I saw that. I was struck by the fact that here is a foretaste of glory divine when we all gather at the Lord's table for His great banquet feast in His presence. He will meet us there. That is His promise for all of us.

One afternoon when I was thirteen, a friend and I went fishing in Godley's Creek, which ran into the Savannah River. We decided to cross the creek at a place where it was not too deep in order to reach a little pool back in the swamp. We had a great time and fished all afternoon. When we started to leave we discovered something we had forgotten. The tide had come in and the creek was up, and we were up the creek. The water was snake-infested, and I was always afraid of snakes. There was only one thing to do. We went across the creek where it had been fairly shallow earlier. I could do it because I knew my father was waiting on me back up at the road on the other side.

Remembering that now I think of the words Jacob spoke to his brother after being gone away for a long time, "To see your face is like seeing the face of God."

Someday we will see the face of God and the faces of all those who have gone before us. They are waiting for us there on the other side.

In the meantime Christ will be meeting us along the way. So, "Do not be afraid. Go and tell my brethren to go to Galilee, and there they will see me."

---

1. Walter L. Underwood, *Being Human Being Hopeful* (Abingdon Press: Nashville, 1987), p. 108.

2. Leslie D. Weatherhead, *After Death* (Abingdon Press: New York, 1936), p. 9.

3. Earl G. Hunt, *I Have Believed* (The Upper Room: Nashville, 1980), p. 147.

4. William Sloane Coffin, *Living The Truth In A World of Illusions* (Harper & Row, Publishers: San Francisco, 1985), p. 71.

5. Robert M. Herhold, *Funny, You Don't Look Christian* (Weybright & Talley: New York, 1969), p. 66.

Morning Prayer
Easter Sunday

O God, as we gather in Thy house today we remember the great, glad, good news, "He is risen." And because of this good news we worship Thee on this glorious Easter Sunday.

With joyful hearts we sing praises to Thy name, and we thank Thee, gracious Father, for this resurrection day, for we know that our lives and the life of all the world have been changed by the resurrection of Thy Son, our Savior Jesus Christ. So, make us Easter people, who always live on this side of Easter. Fill our minds with the wonders of Thy grace, and enable us to be people of victory rather than of defeat, of hope rather than of despair, of faith rather than of fear, of love rather than of hate.

Because of this Easter faith which is ours, call us and lead us ever onward toward greater service for Thee. Lead us to be witnesses of the victory of Thy Son, and guide us toward victorious living in Thy kingdom. Because of this Easter faith, forgive our sins, re-create us in the likeness of Thy Son, and put His love in our hearts.

Bless the witness and service of this congregation as we seek to bring into the lives of people the reality of Easter faith. May all that we do together reflect the goodness, the mercy, the compassion of our Lord and our hope in Him.

Be with and bless people all around us who need Thy presence, Thy help, or the touch of the Master's hand, and guide them through their times of sickness, sorrow and trouble.

Bless Thy people the world over today, and may we all be united in a spirit of service for each other and for Thy kingdom, for we pray today in the name of the King of kings, our resurrected Lord. Amen.

The Best Man Wins

Good morning to all of you! This is Easter Sunday, and I am so glad you are here with us today. This is the day we have been waiting for. This is the day when we celebrate the resurrection of Jesus from death and the tomb.

All of you look so good today. Easter Sunday is the day when we really dress up. Who knows why we do this? It is because we want to wear something new because Jesus has brought new life. This is the good news of our faith.

Look at this Easter egg I have brought with me today. It is very light. Who wants to hold it? See how light it is. It is light because it is empty. We started having Easter eggs at Easter because someone thought that as a chick is born out of the egg so Jesus came out of the tomb. Then someone else came up with the idea of putting a little hole in the egg at both ends and blowing out the contents until the egg is empty. That leaves an empty egg, like the tomb where they put Jesus was empty. This points us to the truth of Easter.

We have a saying we use sometimes, "May the best man win," or "the best man wins." This is what Easter means. Jesus went to Jerusalem to face His enemies. They put Him to death on the cross. But the best man won. That is Jesus. He was the best man. And God won. God and Jesus defeated death and the power of evil.

Do you know what this means for us? It means that God is on our side. It means that when we face hard times God is with us. And it means that when people we love die, God takes them to be with Him. And He will do that for all of us as well. This is the good news of Easter. The best man won, and He is still alive in this world. He is with us and He will always help us.

May we pray. Father, we thank Thee for the good news of Easter and the victory of your Son Jesus Christ. Amen.

Discussion Questions
Easter Sunday

1. Begin with a prayer by a group member.

2. Have someone read Matthew 28:1-10.

3. Having asked them ahead of time, let members of the group share various sections of the chapter.

4. What was the proof of the resurrection of Jesus?

5. What difference did it make in the lives of His followers?

6. Is the resurrection true for you? If so, why?

7. What difference has it made in your life?

8. What will you do about it?

9. Have the group repeat together the Apostles' Creed, followed by a benediction by the leader.

Order Of Worship

11:00 a.m.   **Easter Sunday**

WE GATHER TO WORSHIP GOD
Prelude

Chiming the Hour

Introit

Greeting
Leader: Christ is risen!
People: **He is risen indeed!**

Hymn of Praise   "Christ The Lord Is Risen Today"

Affirmation of Faith   The Apostles' Creed

Welcome and Sharing

Children's Message   "The Best Man Wins"

WE TURN TO GOD IN PRAYER
Joys and Concerns

Morning Prayer and the Lord's Prayer

WE GIVE TO GOD
Prayer of Dedication

Offertory

Doxology

WE HEAR GOD'S WORD
Hymn of Preparation   "Low In The Grave He Lay"

Anthem

Reading of the Scriptures   Matthew 28:1-10
Leader: This is the Word of the Lord.
People: Thanks be to God.

The Message   "The Triumph Of His Defeat"

WE RESPOND TO GOD
The Invitation to Christian Discipleship

Hymn of Invitation   "Crown Him With Many Crowns"

Benediction

Congregational Response

WE DEPART TO SERVE GOD
Postlude